Scotland's East Coast Fishing Ind

By
Mark I'Anson

The Harbour, Port Seton

Back cover & above: Two views of Port Seton Harbour in the 1920s. With the herring industry in a deep depression and so much of the east coast dependent on it, the interwar years were terrible for many fishing communities. In the Lothians, Newhaven and Fisherrow to the west and Dunbar to the east were all suffering dramatic declines. Writing in 1929 Peter Anson praised the fishing folk of Port Seton and Cockenzie for being "an energetic and enterprising race" who alone had managed to "keep going whatever might be the state of the fishing industry".

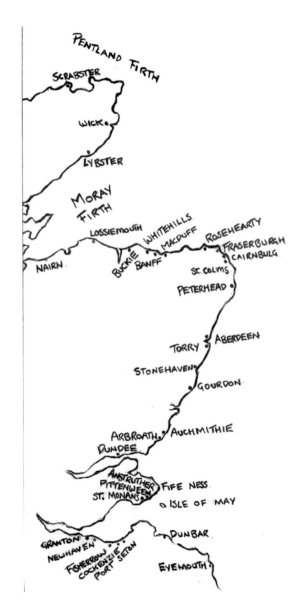

Select Bibliography

Adams, D G, *Auchmithie Home of the Smokie*, Angus District Council 1980s
Anson, P F, *Fishing Boats and Fisher Folk*, J M Dent, London 1930
Anson P F, *Scots Fisher Folk*, Saltire Society 1950
Bochiel, M 'The Fisher Lassies', *The Complete Odyssey*, Billy Kay (Editor), Polygon 1982
Butcher, D, *The Driftermen*, Tops'l Books 1979
Martin, A, *Fishing and Whaling*, National Museums of Scotland 1995
Miller, J, *Salt in the Blood*, Canongate 1999
Samuel, A M, *The Herring*, John Murray, London 1918
Smylie, M, *Herring, A History of the Silver Darlings*, Tempus 2004
Sutherland, I, *Wick Harbour and the Herring Fishery*, Camps Bookshop, Wick 1994
Sutherland, I, *From Herring to Seine Net Fishing*, Camps Bookshop, Wick 1995

Quotes: P. 21 come from 'Harvest of Herring' by J & L Taylor
         P. 22 come from 'Fraserburgh Means Fish' by J & L Taylor
         P. 39 come from 'Recollections of East Fife Fisherfolk' by B Patrick

Acknowledgements

Thanks to Gareth Burgess & Fiona Gebbie, Alex Clark, Sandra Collins, Mike Craine, Linda Fitzpatrick, John Lovie, J Lownie, Shona McMillan, Daniel McPherson, Stuart Marshall, Angus Martin, John More, George Nairn, Joe Reid, Margaret Ritchie, David Sanderson, Betty Slater, Alex Weatherhead, and Malcolm White.

Introduction

Although the fishing industry on the east coast of Scotland is mentioned in records as far back as the 1100s, there is very little documentation of it until the late 1700s. Fishing in small boats, launched out from inlets, bays and beaches all along the coast would mostly have been of a subsistence nature carried out in tandem with crofting for cod, haddock and whiting (all demersal or bottom feeding fish commonly known as white fish). When exactly Scots began to hunt for the herring that would ultimately bring such prosperity to the east coast is unknown. A commercial fishery is recorded at Yarmouth in southeast England around 700 AD, but in Scotland it was not until the twelfth century that a small summer fishery off the Fife coast developed. As this prospered it became known as 'the Lammas Drave' and at its peak in the 1700s was reckoned to involve 20,000 people. That aside, a domestic herring industry in the east was slow to develop although not for want of fish. Each year massive shoals could be seen off the coast with, by all accounts, plenty of boats catching them, but for 500 years these were primarily Dutch boats and the resultant wealth and prosperity went to Holland rather than Scotland. Unsurprisingly Dutch success so close to Scottish shores caused much jealousy and anger. From the 1400s onwards the state began to take a serious interest and started to pass laws, each one attempting to curb the success of the Dutch fleet and/or develop a Scottish fleet. For 300 years these laws failed miserably until finally in 1786 an organisation that would have a huge influence on the future of the Scottish industry was voted into existence. Initially named 'The British Society for Extending the Fisheries and Improving the Sea Coasts of the Kingdom' this was soon afterwards shortened to the 'British Fisheries Society'. It was charged with improving the onshore infrastructure and providing low interest loans to fishermen. Long experienced in catching white fish the Scots, who had through the 1700s began to fish for herring, were hampered by restrictive laws dictating at which harbours they could legally land the herring and the type of salt that had to be used to cure (preserve) the fish. As these laws were gradually lifted and a government bounty (subsidy) was offered on every exported barrel of cured herring, the scene was set for the rapid expansion of the industry. The boom that began in the early 1800s would last almost unabated until the start of the First World War in 1914.

This boom in part coincided with the invention of the camera, now widely accepted as having been invented in 1839. Within five years two pioneering Scots, David Octavius Hill an artist and Robert Adamson a chemist, were using the new invention to photograph the fisherfolk of Newhaven. As photography took hold of the public imagination commercial photographers opened businesses in villages and towns the length and breadth of the country. Some like Alexander Johnston in Wick and George Washington Wilson would continue in Hill and Adamson's footsteps and record the fishing industry. Britain's first picture postcard was published in 1894 and by the early Edwardian period the postcard was taking photographic images of Scottish harbours and ports all round the world. By 1906 750 million picture postcards were being sent through the Royal Mail. Companies such as Valentine & Sons of Dundee covered the Empire, but many of the cards that would later be of such interest to social historians were produced by local photographers and chemists. Within a day or two of any noteworthy local event, whether a village fete, mining disaster or a trawler on the rocks, photographic postcards of the incident might be on sale. The fishing industry, and most especially the herring industry, then enjoying its own heyday, became prime subject matter. Strongly visual, diverse and primarily carried on out of doors, the industry proved perfectly matched to the postcard. Though relatively few postcards exist of life at sea almost every imaginable aspect of harbour life and onshore work seems to be covered somewhere.

Over two thirds of the images in this book are from postcards, the rest a mixture of amateur snaps and press photos. Through these images a north to south journey is followed, from Scrabster to Wick and down to Eyemouth with photos from the late 1800s through to the mid 1970s.

Throughout the 19th century and until 1914 the east coast of Scotland and particularly the town of Wick was seen as synonymous with the herring industry. Yet prior to the late 18th century it had been a large Dutch fleet that each summer fished for herring in the waters surrounding Scotland. It was only in the 1780s that a gradual loosening of prohibitive regulations, combined with government subsidies kick-started the industry. In 1767 Wick had only two herring boats, but by 1790 possessed 32 vessels. The lack of a decent harbour threatened to curtail further expansion, but The British Fisheries Society saw the sheltered bay as the northern location with the greatest potential and purchased land there. Construction of a harbour and accompanying village began in 1803. Initially planned to accommodate 1,000 people such was its success that by 1820 a resident population of 1,500 was being swelled during the herring season to over 5,000 inhabitants with the harbour playing host to 600 boats.

WICK BAY.

THE HARBOUR, WICK.   206998 J.V.

Success followed success. By 1849 author James Thompson could say, as he surveyed an expanse of ground covered with tens of thousands of barrels that "it presents a spectacle not to be met with in this part of the world, if indeed in any other." July and August did bring an incredible industry into the town, but not everyone was quite as impressed. Robert Louis Stevenson wrote to his mother, "Wick in itself possesses no beauty; bare grey shores, grim grey houses, grim grey sea." But if beauty seemed lacking to an outsider, the prosperity brought forth from that grey sea could never be doubted. In 1862 a record fleet of 1,122 boats and 3,800 fishermen used the harbour. In the space of two days, 3,500 fisher girls gutted 50 million herring. Although fleet numbers would diminish from this incredible high, larger more powerful boats would help Wick sustain a fairly constant annual catch until the outbreak of the First World War over 50 years later.

Looking at this view of herring gutters in Wick on a wet September day in 1928 it does not take a great leap of imagination to sense the back-breaking nature of the work, "the most arduous task in the industry", according to the late James Slater, author and fisherman of Portsoy. Long hours were spent leaning over the great wooden troughs, known as farlins, filled with herring. Often, as in George Cormack's yard in the picture above, the women were unprotected from the elements. They were required whatever the weather, to gut and pack every last herring before the boats came in the following morning with fresh loads. What no photo can do justice to is the phenomenal speed with which these women worked. An experienced worker could gut 60 to 70 herring a minute. Throat slit, gills and intestines pulled out (sold later to farmers for fertilizer) and fish slung, instinctively graded by size, into one of several tubs, or 'croosies' behind her. A full day's work could see a single gutter get through up to between 15,000 and 20,000 fish.

Right: The girls worked in teams of three, one packer to every two gutters. Together they would rouse the gutted fish in salt and then began the skilled work of the packer. Under the watchful eyes of the coopers she would carefully place the herring, silver belly upwards, in layers, interspersed with handfuls of salt. It was claimed that in a well-packed barrel each layer should remain in place, even if the surrounding structure of the barrel was removed. Fully packed they would be left to settle. As the salt drew moisture out of them the herring would sink down. Barrels would then be reopened and topped up with similarly sized and cured fish. Finally containing between 700 and 1,000 fish they would be filled with pickle then inspected by a Fishery Officer and if all was in order, the barrel would receive an official crown brand and be sealed ready for export. Coopers (400 were employed in Wick alone), who out of season would make the barrels, were responsible for overseeing the girls' work. High standards were demanded by buyers who would open at random the finished barrels to check the quality of the product.

This postcard of Lybster Harbour twelve miles south of Wick, was posted to Miss Bessie Irvine in New York City on 19 July 1907. While accepting that the Big Apple was rather more basic 100 years ago, it is still hard to imagine two more different environments. Yet Lybster too had its heyday. A wooden jetty built in 1810 to help local crofters supplement their income by fishing was so successful that the substantial stone harbour seen below replaced it in 1830. Bustling with boats and curers' yards it could soon claim to be Scotland's third herring port, behind only Wick and Fraserburgh. Before long though, new and bigger boats were congregating in the larger ports. First to suffer were tiny harbours such as Clyth and Whaligoe just to the north of Lybster. Initially Lybster held on and in 1881 was still home to 129 boats but within fifteen years the number was down to 50 and by the 1920s only seventeen small boats remained. Nowadays a few inshore boats use this fine harbour which remains in good repair. A new quay was added in 1984 and disused harbour buildings have been renovated and reborn as a visitors centre.

While the first experimental steam drifters may have been built in Scotland in the late 1870s it was only around the turn of the century that they began to be widely recognised as a viable alternative to sail. Moray Firth fishermen, widely recognised and respected for their innovation and progressiveness, embraced them with open arms. Soon yards all along the Moray coast, that had previously been engaged in building sailing vessels, switched to steamers. The first of thirty to arrive in Nairn was the *Hope (INS138)* in 1906. The harbour there had been built in 1820 for 40ft sailing boats and was quite unable to cope with the 85ft drifters. For many years the fleet had to tie up in Inverness when not at sea. Constant badgering by frustrated fishermen finally forced the town council to approve plans for a new harbour basin in the late 1920s, which was opened in 1932. Identifiable among the local drifters tied up there in 1933 are (from the right) *Brighton o' the North (INS382)*, *Nairnside (INS296)*, *Mistress Isa (INS399)* and *Glenerne (INS27)*.

At one time many people believed that a massive shoal of herring arrived from 'far away', migrated round the British Isles and returned to 'far away'. In fact there were several completely separate stocks gathering in large shoals and moving in towards land each year to spawn. It was on these grounds that the great herring fisheries grew up, with the ports closest benefiting most from the seasonal bonanza. Lerwick became a major centre between May and August, Stronsay and Wick around the same time while Fife enjoyed a winter fishery from January to March. In the early years of the 19th century fishing communities would only forsake traditional line fishing (for haddock and cod) and turn to the herring when they were close by. However, as the century progressed and boats became larger they began to venture further afield, spending more and more time on the herring and only returning home for brief periods between seasons. The year now culminated in autumn in East Anglia when a thousand and more Scottish drifters could be fishing from Great Yarmouth and Lowestoft.

Women have always had a central role in fisher life, at the very heart of the community, doing all the onshore jobs that made the work at sea possible. With the arrival of the herring industry their role was to change. As gutters and packers they were required to be where the fish were and as the boats followed the herring, so the women also followed the boats. The journeying started in early May, often with the dreaded overnight sailing to Lerwick, when all but the lucky few suffered acute seasickness. For others, the destination might be Stronsay, Fraserburgh or Wick while some went west to Mallaig or down to the Isle of Man and across to Ireland. August heralded the end of the summer seasons and a brief return home before the journey to East Anglia began. Special trains ran to Yarmouth, but some of the many thousands heading south would gradually work their way down the east coast. Seahouses (seen below circa 1910), Blyth, North Shields, Hartlepool, Whitby, Scarborough and Grimsby would all see brief annual influxes of Scottish boats and girls on their way to the great 'sooth' fishing.

Though its origins are now lost in time, Dutch fishermen had perfected the drift net by the end of the 15th century and it was to remain largely unchanged (apart from its length) throughout its long history. Essentially it was a curtain of nets hanging down in the water stretching, at its peak in the early 20th century, for up to two miles while the vessel to which it was attached drifted with the tide. Pelagic fish, such as herring and mackerel, live near the seabed, at depths down to 250 metres, only rising to feed as night falls. With the drift nets being shot at dusk (as in the picture above) the hope of all driftermen is that as the herring rise they will swim into the net and become caught by the gills. The great risk, especially in the days before echo sounders was that the fish simply were not there and nights could be spent hauling empty nets. Then hopefully, in the words of poet and writer Angus Martin, himself an ex fisherman "The labours of one night would redeem the long wait; a big catch sold at a good price and fantastic wealth in the pockets of the crew."

Whereas before WW1 empty nets had been the main concern, the big worry from 1921 onwards was a glut of herring with no buyers in sight. Men who had spent long hours during the night hauling in nets full of fish found themselves in the soul-destroying and poverty-inducing position of steaming back out to spend the afternoon dumping the catch overboard. Often, as in the picture of Yarmouth above, the fleet would remain tied up rather than catch unsaleable fish. Men's livelihoods were being destroyed by events far from the fishing grounds and totally outwith their control. An industry that, prior to 1914, had seemed invincible and eternal, collapsed almost overnight as it lost its two main markets. Russia, which had taken a million barrels a year was, following the 1917 Revolution, seen by the British Government as a dangerous opponent and all trade with it discouraged. Germany, struggling to stave off post-war starvation initially outbid all other customers, but as its economy went into meltdown through 1922/23 so its purchasing power disintegrated. Though Scotland's herring industry would limp on for a further 40 years it would only do so in a much diminished form.

THE HARBOUR, LOSSIEMOUTH

History credits Lossiemouth innovator William 'Dad' Campbell with designing the Zulu fishing boat. Prior to his invention there were two general types of fishing craft common on the east coast. The Scaffie, popular on the south of the Moray Firth, had a curved stem and sharply raked stern, giving a short keel in relation to its overall length. This made for an easily manoeuvrable boat suitable for launching from open beaches. The second type was the Fifie with a near vertical stem and stern giving a heavy powerful fast and stable boat. Legend has it that Campbell's Zulu design originated in a family argument. He was for the Scaffie, while his wife, from Cairnbulg near Fraserburgh, favoured the Fifie. Their compromise, combining the straight stem of the Fifie with the raked stern of a Scaffie, was launched on 7 December 1879 and aptly named the 'Nonesuch'. The successful design quickly spread. Within four years there were over 3,500 of these boats registered in Scotland and rather bizarrely nicknamed Zulus after the Zulu Wars then taking place in South Africa and grabbing the headlines in Britain.

FISH MARKET, LOSSIEMOUTH (PHOTO- I.M. MATHESON, LOSSIEMOUTH)

Scots driftermen on their annual journey southwards in 1921 saw for the first time Danish seine net boats fishing out of Hull and Grimsby. The herring industry was mired in deep depression and progressive Moray Firth skippers were open to any new ideas. With 75% of Lossiemouth boats making a loss that year radical measures were needed just for survival. While some drifters tried trawling, others began to experiment with the seine net, both hunting whitefish rather than herring. The seine net was cheaper and lighter than the trawl net and in comparison it was mobile; shooting and hauling could be completed within the hour and if unsuccessful, new fishing grounds could then be sought out. At first viewed as winter back-up to herring fishing, the seine net steadily took over. Lossiemouth skippers were among the earliest to adopt the method and it was a local man, John Campbell, nephew of William 'dad' Campbell, who in 1927 became the first Scot to launch a vessel, the *Marigold (INS234)*, designed solely for seine net fishing. Later seiners, following his innovative example, can be seen in this 1950s photo.

In 1929 Buckie remained home to 290 steam drifters, the largest fleet in Scotland. Seine netting had been carried out west and east along the Moray coast for eight years while motorboats, being cheaper to run, had outnumbered steamers since 1915. Alone the Buckie men had persisted in large numbers through the lean years of the 1920s with their drifters. Some had been fitted out for trawling and some for the seine net. In neither case were the drifters ideal, being too large and costly to run for seining and lacking enough engine power to be truly successful trawlers. They were damp, basic and uncomfortable to work on, yet they are fondly remembered, described by one fisherman as 'the most beautiful boat ever built for the job'. By the late 1920s though they were prohibitively expensive to run, chasing depleted stocks for a depressed market. Within ten years drifters that had sold for around £5,000 in 1919 could be had ready to fish for £40. Hundreds were sold for scrap, many fishermen emigrated or left the industry, and a way of life passed into history.

WHITEHILLS HARBOUR

An article in the Scots Magazine around the time of this 1960s postcard describes Whitehills as possessing "a fleet of 30 boats each with a crew of four born in the parish". Fishing in the Moray Firth these boats would return for the daily sales in the fish market, the gable end of which is just visible to the left hand side of the photo. This tidy harbour was built in 1900 as a 'Trust Harbour', owned by the community, maintained and run on their behalf by nine locally elected commissioners. It remains as such, though in 1999 with much regret the commissioners decided that, with ever more draconian regulations leading to a reduction in fishing fleet size, the only way to secure the future of their harbour was to develop it as a marina. The influence of fishing though is still keenly felt. The last boat to actually land fish was the *Budding Rose (BF156)* in 2004, but about fifteen skippers still live in the village, while basing their boats in larger harbours, primarily Macduff of Edinburgh.

HARBOUR, BANFF.

Left: The fickle nature of changing fortunes in the fishing industry is well illustrated by looking at the contrasting histories of the Moray Firth neighbours, Banff and Macduff. Banff has a long and proud maritime history traceable back to the 14th century when continental trade with the Baltic and Mediterranean ports flourished. Within seven years of the herring industry being established here, in 1815, ninety boats were fishing from the harbour. In the 1830s around 30,000 barrels of herring were being cured annually for export but midway through the century a change in the course of the River Deveron, as it flows into the bay between the two towns, caused Banff Harbour to begin to silt up. The larger trading boats could no longer use the port and many of the bigger fishing boats started to work from Macduff. Ownership of these boats remained in the town and in the late 1920s a fleet of seventeen steam drifters could still be seen filling Banff Harbour between fishing seasons. No herring were being landed though and 80 years later the place has a distinctly 'olde world' feel, the largely deserted quays remaining almost unaltered in the 100 years since this photo was taken.

Above: In stark contrast, a mile across the bay lies 'Macduff - a working harbour'. This slogan is no mere sound bite. Provost Bill Howatson recently estimated that 36% of all jobs in the town are linked to the sea. Behind this modern success story lies 200 years of developments and improvements. The harbour was originally built around 1770 when two basins, east and west, were constructed. Major developments occurred in the 1820s, 1870s and again in 1902/1903 and 1921 when the construction of the Princess Royal Basin finally obliterated 'Rob Laing's Pier'. This jetty, seen above, predated even the 1770s harbour. More recently a fish market was opened in 1955 only to be replaced by a more modern one just ten years later. Perhaps today Macduff is better known for its busy shipbuilding and repair facilities. In August 2008 a state of the art ship lift, costing £3.9m, has replaced the old slipway. Like their harbour Macduff fishermen have adapted and changed, embracing first the herring fishery then following closely their Lossiemouth counterparts in the use of the seine nets and more recently concentrating on trawling.

Smiling faces in old black and white photos and reminiscences concluding with "Ach! It was still the best days of my life." They seem almost surreal to 21st century sensibilities when the subject involved is the gutting and packing of seemingly endless herring. Margaret Bochel, born into a Nairn fishing family in the 1920s , remembered, "Living conditions were primitive, the pay was miserable and the work exhausting... however the girls eagerly looked forward to and greatly enjoyed the gutting." Starting out around the age of fifteen, usually under the watchful eyes of elder sisters or friends, girls would spend their first season learning on the job. The curers for whom they worked took no responsibility for training them. Paid on a piecework basis, regularly putting in fifteen hour days, often far from home, it was hard repetitive work. Lassies (of all ages) and from many different places found a sense of independence and self-assurance as together they followed the drifters on their annual migration down the east coast to Yarmouth. Friendships made at the gutting would often last a lifetime.

Problems though did sometimes arise. Usually, but not always, these disputes were about lack of pay and culminated in strikes in the East Anglian autumn. The girls were, in the words of the Gaelic poet Derick Thomson "slaves to short arsed curers". "We were working in October and November with snow and frost on the ground. There was nothing abeen yer head! No covering at all and we stood there rain or shine... and a'that for 10d a barrel 'etween three o' us." This was on top of the (very) basic pay of 15/- a week, from which half went straight to landladies to pay for lodgings. The girls were left with little option but to strike. "It'd cam to the p'int that we were working for Pandrops." Perhaps the largest and best remembered dispute was led by Mary Gatt of Rosehearty. Fellow striker, Nellie Blair, recalling a strike between the wars remembered, "I can hear her yet with the sound of her powerful voice ringing in my lug as she shouted 'All out for more money; all out for more pay!'" The women came out and stayed out, finally together winning their raise after a week long strike.

Throughout the 19th century Fraserburgh was an exceptionally successful herring port, second only in Scotland to Wick. The turn of the century saw a change as steam began to replace sail. Fishermen from the Broch were slow to change until a report in the local press in the spring of 1906 showed profits for the previous season to be three times greater for the steamers. A sudden flood of orders left the three local shipbuilders struggling to cope. Wilson Noble & Co, whose yard was too small to deal with 85 foot boats, managed finally to lease a new site in October 1906 and it is from that yard, as yet uncovered, that the *Gowan (FR232)* is seen being launched just a few months later. Local fisherman Jim Buchan, remembering these times of change, quoted a contemporary saying "In the sail boats it was iron men and wooden boats because everything was done by hand. When the steam drifter arrived it was iron boats and wooden men as everything was done by machinery"!

Europe's top fishing port in 2007 with record landings worth £108m, Peterhead has always relied on the harvest of the seas for its prosperity. A first basic harbour, known as Port Henry, was established in the 1590s. In the late 18th century whaling began and the town grew to be the country's main port for Arctic whalers before a steady decline saw the last one leave in 1893. But by then the harbour was an established herring port. A record 849 boats are said to have fished from here in 1881. The arrival of steam power was embraced. By the outbreak of WW1, 196 steamers bore the PD registration though in season the number of vessels using the harbour could far exceed that. The post-war years saw major investment in modern seine netters. These were then eclipsed by the phenomenal growth of the white fish fleet as many boats moved north from Aberdeen in the 1970s/1980s. Changing as the industries changed in the last fifteen years, a massive ongoing development centred on the deepwater quays has attracted some of Europe's largest pelagic vessels to land their catches here.

Kippered or fresh, the herring is a tremendous source of nutrients. Mrs Hedrikje van Andel Schipper who, prior to her death at the age 115, was the world's oldest person, put her health and longevity down to eating a herring a day. While such long life cannot be guaranteed the health-giving properties of herring are unquestionable. High in Omega 3 oils that can guard against heart disease and help reduce the effects of arthritis it is also full of vitamins A & D, high in protein and rich in minerals. Yet in a modern Britain more obsessed than ever with food and health the herring is a distinctly unfashionable fish. Much of those landed in Scotland today are processed into fishmeal and animal feed. Author Mike Smylie calls it "an absolutely crazy situation" and is confident that if the British public could be persuaded to eat herring twice a week our health would improve and the strain on the NHS decrease. Even more emphatically The Herring Industry Board, on behalf of the government, claimed in 1975 "If all of us ate only 25 herring and 25 kippers in a year... we would be a great deal healthier and wealthier too"!

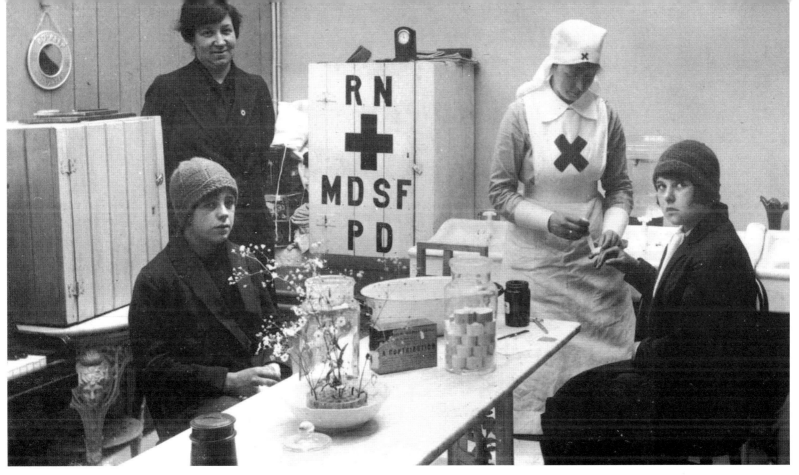

While working at the gutting every morning, the girls would tear strips of cotton, often from flour bags bought from the bakers and bind each finger individually to protect them. These 'clooties' would remain on all day but, despite the protection, cuts were common, due in great part to the exceptional speed with which the girls worked. Cuts and sores would then be aggravated by the constantly recurring contact with salt and brine. Dressing stations such as this one in Peterhead provided by The Royal National Mission to Deep Sea Fishermen (RNMDSF) provided welcome relief. The Mission was founded in 1881 by Ebenezer Mather following a trip to the North Sea fishing grounds. Appalled by the conditions he saw the men working under, he returned home, raised money, purchased a second-hand fishing smack, the 'Ensign', and set to work providing the men with support, both material and spiritual. The organisation went from strength to strength, constantly developing to serve fisher folk in an ever-changing industry. In 2006 it celebrated its 125th anniversary "Providing emergency & welfare support to fishermen and their families 24 hours a day, 7 days a week, 365 days a year."

The re-routing of the River Dee and the building of a new south breakwater (visible on the right of photo) were instrumental in solving Aberdeen's problems of a treacherous harbour entrance and poor quayside facilities. These had seriously limited the growth of the towns fishing industry prior to the 1870s. There then followed a decade of steady growth with over 400 herring boats (similar to those above) using the harbour facilities each year. However, nothing could prepare the locals for the sudden white fish boom that would begin here in 1882. Trawling, where a large bag-like net is towed along the sea bed to catch demersal fish, such as cod, haddock and plaice, had benefited most from the introduction of steam power during the 1870s. From its inception it had been greeted with great hostility by driftnet men who saw this new technique as a threat to fish stocks and thus to their livelihoods. In Wick a visiting trawler crew were stoned as they mended their nets on the quayside, but when two English trawlers landed catches in Aberdeen in 1882 local businessmen were impressed enough to try out this new method for themselves, initially using the steam tug *Toiler*. Success prompted two new builds, the *North Star* and the *Gypsy*, which were launched the following year, and by 1900 there were 148 steam trawlers registered in the city. Large powerful boats like those seen to the right entering Aberdeen Harbour were able to tow bigger nets. No longer reliant on the wind they could go further and faster covering larger areas of the seabed, catching greater numbers of fish. They brought great prosperity to the town, summed up with typical Aberdonian forthrightness in the local expression that the wealth 'Aa cam oot o' a cod's airse'. For many years Aberdeen was the third largest fishing port in Britain behind Hull and Grimsby. Throughout the 1950s the steamers were gradually replaced by diesel boats. Cheaper to run and better for their crews to work aboard, they had greater catching power and were able to sustain the port's success until the collapse of the industry in the mid 1970s following the Cod Wars with Iceland. By then many trawlermen had seen the writing on the wall and switched to well-paid jobs in the booming oil industry.

Traditionally Scottish fishing boats were jointly owned, often within families. The men who sailed them and the women who saw to the work on shore all had a vital stake in their boats. Trawling, right from its inception, was different with vessels primarily owned by companies. Often these grew to be very large operations owning many boats. For fishing communities it became a case of the 'haves and have nots', the owners and the workers. Wages were squeezed to increase the owners' incomes and a poundage system was introduced, whereby the men would receive a tiny percentage of the profits. Having to pay the company for food and provisions it was not unknown to return from a gruelling four week trip and find the men owing the owners money. Conditions did improve with time. After disputes, food was paid for by the companies and the men earned a basic wage with some benefits if the catch was good. It remained though a hard and dangerous way to earn a living, long hours of work taking place on open decks, often in conditions unimaginable to those on land.

Right: The Aberdeen vessel *Keith Hall (A636)* had a varied and unusual career before coming to grief on Orkney. Built in Germany in 1896 as the trawler *Darmstadt*, she was renamed *Carbosin* following capture by *HMS Cleopatra* on 30th September 1915. One of 27 German trawlers caught during WW1 and converted for use by the British Navy, these boats became known as 'C-Sin' trawlers. After the war she was sold to Aberdeen owners Ellis & Meff, renamed the *Keith Hall* and embarked on a short career as a great liner. On the evening of Sunday 27 November 1921, when returning home from the Faroes, she ran aground in fog at Skifigoe, near Birsay on the west of the Orkney mainland. While helping to launch the small boat, crewman George Neilson from Torry was swept overboard and drowned. The rest of the crew were picked up safely by the Stromness lifeboat.

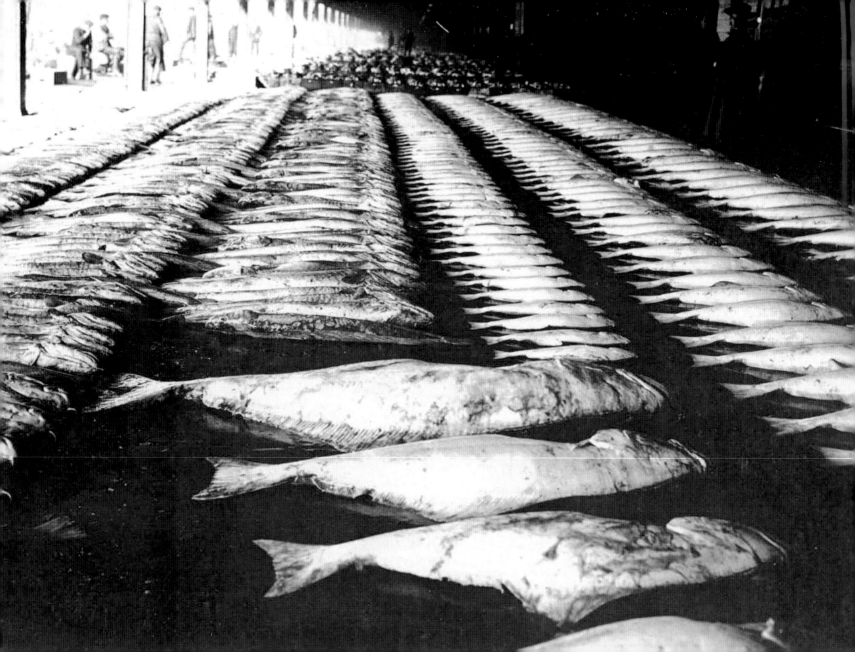

Line caught cod and halibut, graded by size and laid out awaiting auction in Aberdeen Fish Market. Before the advent of steam trawlers all white fish caught in Scotland would have been by line from boats, normally fishing within twenty miles of the land. The arrival of steam power and the rapid increase in vessel size and strength changed all this. Soon great liners, like the *Keith Hall* (page 29), would be steaming as far as Greenland in search of halibut. Cod and ling could be found off the Faroes and Iceland. Lines could now stretch for several miles with hundreds of hooks and, although trawlers could land bigger catches, line caught fish tended to be larger and, undamaged by trawl nets, they attracted premium prices. The arrival in the 1960s of modern motor trawlers, able in ten days to outfish and outearn a four week liner trip, signalled the end of great lining in Aberdeen. Recent years though have seen a renewed interest throughout the UK in line caught fish as a sustainable and ecologically friendly fishery.

Right: The vast majority of Britain's steam fishing fleet was pressed into service in both World Wars performing with great success a multitude of different tasks. Here trawlermen are holding up large cod, caught in December 1941 while on a break from minesweeping duties in the North Sea. Cod has been an important food since prehistoric times, fished on a commercial scale throughout the northern hemisphere since at least the 11th century. Now through overfishing and perhaps affected by the warming of the seas, cod is considered by scientists to be an endangered species and fishing in the North Sea is severely restricted. Surveys are undertaken to allow estimates of cod stocks to be made. Sustainable targets are set and total allowable catches (TACs) are changed from year to year. British fishermen though, who have seen dramatic increases in cod numbers in their nets in recent years, feel their practical experience is being ignored by scientists and politicians. That being said, the TAC for North Sea cod for 2008, after many years of decreases, has finally been increased by 11%.

STONEHAVEN
HARBOUR 1062   G M MILLER

Prior to the successful development of Aberdeen Harbour, Stonehaven had been the main fishing station between Peterhead and Anstruther. The harbour, seen above at the start of the 20th century, looks fairly busy with around 50 boats in it. Yet just forty years earlier, during the herring season there could easily be 200 boats crammed in. In 1871 a total of 230, including many foreign vessels, fished from the town. Such could be the chaos that the Harbour Board introduced a set of rules. Each curer was limited to just one ton of salt and 50 empty barrels on the pier. All filled barrels had to be removed immediately and clear passage left along the quayside. By 1900 quaysides were deserted and such rules were unnecessary, though many of the postcards produced around this time show a still vibrant, if ageing fishing community living and working around the harbour. Legend has put the demise of Stonehaven (and that of Dunbar) down to the men from both ports fishing on Sundays, thus desecrating the Sabbath. Commonsense, however, indicates that for Stonehaven at least proximity to Aberdeen has been the problem.

In March 1928 a 'Press and Journal' study into 'the decay in fishing villages', found just two places to be bucking the trend, Arbroath and Gourdon. They alone seemed to have survived the bleak 1920s and were reckoned to have recaptured their pre-war prosperity. Both were tight-knit communities that had kept to the traditional sma' line method of fishing. Hunting for haddock, whiting and flounders they had been far less affected by the collapse of the herring industry. Elsewhere young men returning from the trenches with changed expectations had rejected the role of deckhands on the bigger boats and opted instead to leave the industry or emigrate. Having resisted the temptations of the steamers and continued instead with their small family-owned boats, the fishermen of Gourdon had vessels to pass down the generations keeping the youngsters in the village and the industry. When this photo was taken, around 1932, there were 150 men and 39 boats working out of Gourdon and couples such as William and Hannah Lownie, to the right of the picture, were bringing up their families within a vibrant fishing community.

Walter Scott visited Auchmithie in 1814 and proceeded to immortalise the locals as the 'Mucklebackits of Musselcraig'. In the novel 'The Antiquary' he has Maggie Mucklebackit explain *"If the men do the work at sea we maun surely tak the work ashore"*. This was no easy task. On top of all domestic and child-rearing duties, the work involved in preparing the lines for the next day's fishing was a full-time job in itself. A sma' line with 1200 to 1400 hooks required around 2,000 mussels and these needed to be shelled daily. Often on winter mornings the women would be up by 4 a.m., with cloths tied round their fingers for protection, hard at work shelling mussels. The previous day's line (each fisherman owned two lines) would have been cleaned of seaweed, starfish and old bait and any missing or broken hooks replaced. Now it was baited with the newly-shelled mussels, up to two per hook, before being skilfully arranged in a long wicker basket known as a 'scull' (see photo on page 33) ready for the next day's fishing.

Nearly thirty years before Walter Scott, Robert Burns had visited Auchmithie, the first in a long line of literary tourists to pass through and often write about the village. In their footsteps came photographers, many from the nearby towns of Arbroath and Dundee, and it is them we have to thank for one of the best visual records of late Victorian fisher life in Scotland. The picture to the right of Tam Swankie, hands on knees, watching his mother and wife, Leebie, was taken by Councillor Walter Ankorn, a commercial photographer in Arbroath who published a number of postcards of Auchmithie. While written descriptions abound of the women putting shoulders and backs into the task of launching the boats, this is the only photographic record of it that I have seen. As well as barefootedly launching the boats the women, to ensure their men would start the day dry shod, would carry husbands and sons on their shoulders out into the icy North Sea to the boats with, according to one eyewitness "the greatest of ease and all nonchalance imaginable"! On their return it is said that the women would again enter the water sometimes up to their necks, to guide the boats safely home.

Dividing their Catch. Auchmithie

Once ashore the fish would be divided out and loaded into creels, known locally as ripps. With these hoisted on their backs the women carried the heavy loads up the steep hill to the village. There the fresh haddock were gutted and prepared for smoking, salted, tied by their tails in pairs, then left to dry for two to three hours. Once dry, the fish were suspended from wooden bars over a sunken half-barrel containing a dampened down smokey fire. Wet canvas sacking was used as a cover and the fish left to cook in the smoke for around 45 minutes. Ripps would then be filled with the cooked 'smokies', a second smaller basket called a murlin full of fresh fish added on top and the women were ready to set off on their rounds. They would walk the surrounding countryside, sometimes covering huge distances selling their fish (the 40 mile round trip to Dundee was not unheard of). Such incredibly hard work produced generations of strong, self-confident and independent women and although unusual for the Victorian era, their word, in the home at least, tended to be the law.

D G Adam in 'Auchmithie, Home of the Smokie' notes how "In periods of relative wealth and good herring seasons fisher weddings saw the groom dressed in claw hammer jaicket and lum hat." The wedding pictured above would have been taking place on a Friday, probably in September, with the season just finished. The bride and her attendants, the 'best maid' and the 'warst maid' wore fashionable dresses which afterwards were kept for Sunday best. In fisher communities like Authmithie weddings were the main source of festivity and recreation. Large quantities of alcohol could be consumed which led the Kirk Session in Buckie to demand a pledge of half a guinea beforehand to ensure no rioting or fighting, the money being either returned the following Sunday or given to the poor. In Auchmithie it was a custom on the morning of the wedding for the groom to send his bride a gift of two purses. They were made to last a lifetime and while being practical were also symbolic of the wife's role in charge of their money. Marriage in such communities was a partnership of equals.

THE HARBOUR FROM EAST, ARBROATH.

A.5391.

Though Arbroath has had a harbour since at least the 14th century, records show that by the early 1700s there was still little fishing industry to speak of. In 1705 the town council, keen to develop one, are said to have offered incentives to Auchmithie fishermen to move the 3? miles along the coast. Robert and James Cargill with their families, boats and gear took up the offer. The 'owner' of Auchmithie, Lord Northesk, was less than amused and proceeded to take the men and the Arbroath Town Magistrates to court in Edinburgh. He won his claim that the fisherfolk were, like the salters and colliers, still serfs unable under the law to move when and where they wished. It would take another 94 years before these repressive laws were repealed and a further 27 until the Arbroath councillors found the courage to once more try to attract Auchmithie residents. Their subsequent success has bequeathed to the town a lasting legacy. Not only do the five most common fisher names in the town, Cargill, Spink, Beattie, Swankie and Smith all originate in the tiny village of Auchmithie, but they brought the smokie, now the 'Arbroath Smokie' with them.

Between the wars, just off the Fife coast, in grounds stretching from Elie Ness to Fife Ness, a winter herring fishery prospered. As it developed boats came from the north and buyers from the south. Quaysides which, from October to December, had lain empty (with local boats away at 'the sooth' fishery) now clamoured with activity. In 1930 ring net boats from the Clyde first appeared. The drift net men, especially those from St. Monans, feared the newcomers would fish the Forth dry. With drifters and ring netters in such close proximity (both can be seen above leaving Anstruther for the fishing grounds) and with the fishing taking place during the night, incidents were frequent and tensions ran high. In the 1934 season alone, 69 drift nets were allegedly lost and 417 damaged with 98 complaints being made to the Fishing Board. Over several years the antagonisms declined and relations improved. Disputes aside, this was the most important time of the year for the local communities and a vital source of income. In the words of Belle Patrick, born in Anstruther in 1895, *"If money did not come in through the harbour mouth it did not come in at all."*

In 1929 when Peter Anson wrote his acclaimed book 'Fishing Boats & Fisher Folk', the Fife village of Pittenweem merited barely a mention, sandwiched between the then bustling harbours of St. Monans and Anstruther. Today it is Fife's premier fishing centre. Like Port Seton across the Forth, modern Pittenweem is reliant almost exclusively on shellfish for its income. In 2007 out of a total catch worth £3.6m, £3.1m came from shellfish and of that £2.6m was for prawns (also known as nephrops or langoustine). This would have been quite unbelievable in 1929 and not just because of the inflated values (Pittenweem's total catch in 1928 was worth £16,000) but also because, prior to the upsurge in popularity of scampi (prawn tails) in the 1950s, there had been no market for prawns at all and fishermen catching them would have been liable to throw them back into the sea. Indeed the town's post-war success had been built not on shellfish but on white fish. The newly-built seiner 'Constant Hope II' can be seen in this 1975 photo. These days though, prawns are the single most important and valuable species landed in Scotland, without which the industry would be in dire straits.

The home fleet in the English port of North Shields consisted mainly of steam trawlers hunting the North Sea for cod, but each August and September there would be an influx of, mainly Scottish, drifters following the herring shoals. The fish quay, seen above in 1910, could be packed solid with a mixture of sail and steam boats while the quaysides would fill with temporary curers' yards. The Scottish connection can be glimpsed in this photo with all four of the identifiable boats either made in or belonging to Fife. Three of them, the North Shields drifter *Redvers Buller (SN297)* (extreme left), the *Christina Mayes (ML123)* of St. Monans next to it, and the *Merganser (A740)* from Aberdeen were all built in the Anstruther yard of the famous St. Monans boatbuilder J N Miller & Sons. The fourth boat the *Edith (KY460)*, though built in Leith, belonged to Anstruther. Both Fife registered boats would be lost off their home coast. The *Edith* wrecked on the Isle of May on 8 September 1924 while the *Christina Mayes*, by now renamed *Mare Vivimus (KY98)*, would sink off Elie Ness just over 15 months later on 12 December 1925.

AUCTIONING HERRING AT ST. MONANS.   98748.JV.

Christopher Rush, author of 'A Twelvemonth and a Day', was born in St. Monans in 1944 and recalls growing up in a town dominated by fishing, religion and strong matriarchs. The pulpit above may be for the selling of fish rather than the preaching of the word yet religion has traditionally been an immensely important element in the lives of many ordinary fisher folk. Two great revival movements brought a fervour in fishing communities perhaps more regularly associated with religion in the USA than in Presbyterian Scotland. The first in 1859, centred on Peterhead while the second took place during the Yarmouth fishing in autumn 1921. This had a huge effect as converted fishermen, many with evangelical zeal, returned to their own communities. Even thirty years later, as a child growing up, Rush could remember ten different denominations serving a population of 1,000. Aside from the Church of Scotland and the Catholic Church the good folk of St. Monans could attend worship with the Congregationalists, the Salvation Army and several different groups of Brethren. Not without cause was St. Monans (named after a local saint reputedly martyred on the May Island) known, throughout Fife, as 'The Holy City'.

LEAVING FOR THE FISHING GROUNDS. ST. MONANCE. 6212

From the start of the 20th century paraffin oil motors had been tested in fishing boats. By 1907, with initial teething problems sorted out, the scene was set for the rapid mechanisation of the Scottish fleet. As steam had replaced sail, just as the large sailing boats seemed to be reaching perfection, so motorboats began to replace the steamers in the very midst of their heyday. Following a decade of frantic boatbuilding, by 1911 Scotland had nearly 800 steamers but within four short years they would be outnumbered by motorboats. By the late 1920s in St. Monans alone the 44 motorboats would outnumber steamers by four to one. It had proved simple and cost-effective to add motors to the traditional sailing boats. A motor could be bought for around £200 whereas a steamer could cost £3,000 to £4,000, and the savings did not stop with construction; the motorboats were also far more economical to run. With running costs dramatically reduced and with smaller crews of only five or six to divide the profits between (as opposed to ten men on a steam drifter), the ordinary fishermen's income rose significantly.

With easy access to the Lothian coalfields and Edinburgh on its doorstep, after the arrival of its first steam trawler in 1885 Granton Harbour quickly became Scotland's second trawler port. Special trains left daily for Glasgow and by the late 1920s half the catch was heading to the west. In the early 1950s the harbour still retained a fleet of 44 steamers although most had been built before WW1. With the cost of coal rising and catches on the whole declining, they were ceasing to be financially viable. Stricter safety regulations added further costs. From the mid 1950s they began to be replaced by diesel trawlers with better facilities for the men and far superior technology, equipment and catching power. Boats such as the *Granton Osprey (GN19)* fished from the port through the 1960s and early 1970s until the sudden decline of the white fish industry around 1975 brought 130 years of fishing from Granton to an end. Many of the boats, like the *Osprey*, went on to work as offshore standby vessels. Renamed *Putford Osprey* she worked from Lowestoft until 1993 when she was sold to new owners in Lisbon.

M. F. V. "FAIRTRY II"

Though vessels like the *Granton Osprey* were a big improvement, they still fished in a similar way to the steamers, the nets being shot and hauled over the side. In the late 1940s a group of businessmen, noticing that in the Antarctic whalers pulled their catch up a stern ramp, began experimenting on the Clyde. First they used a converted steam yacht, the *Oriana*, then an adapted minesweeper *HMS Felicity*. Renamed the *Fairtree (LH371)* she was to become the world's first combined freezer/stern trawler. Christian Salvesen of Leith purchased her and, after teething problems, had great success. In 1954 a purpose-built replacement *Fairtry (LH8)* was launched in Aberdeen. At 280ft long she was the largest fishing vessel of her time and represented the very latest in technology. For ordinary fishermen she was a great leap forward in safety. No longer was the work of sorting and gutting the catch done in the open; now it all took place under deck in factory-like conditions. *Fairtry* was followed in 1959 by *Fairtry II* (pictured) and by *Fairtry III (LH371)*. Nearly all future freezer stern trawlers the world over would be modelled, to a degree, on these innovative Scottish boats.

When Edinburgh's connection to fishing is talked of, people automatically think of Newhaven and fishwives. But it was another less remembered aspect rather that was perhaps the area's most important contribution to the industry. Without efficient nets precious few herring would have been caught and though the Dutch may have invented the drift net it was a son of Musselburgh, James Patterson, who is credited with developing a mechanical loom for the manufacture of nets. Lowestoft writer, David Butcher, describing Patterson's invention reckons that "This may have been the most crucial development in drift net fishing throughout its long history." Patterson formed a company in 1820 using his new machine just as Scotland's herring industry was beginning to flourish. Initial problems in producing knots that wouldn't slip were resolved by Leither, Walter Ritchie, and gradually machine nets replaced the old handmade ones. By 1869 Scotland had fourteen factories manufacturing nets and employing over 2,000 people. Despite the machinery the use of handheld netting needles, such as can be seen in this 1916 photo from Newhaven, continued (and continues) to be needed for repairing, altering and finishing off even the most hi-tech modern nets.

Though perhaps less famous with the general public than their Newhaven counterparts, there can be no doubting the uniqueness of the Fisherrow women. Historically their feats of speed, while carrying on their backs loaden creels from Fisherrow up into the centre of Edinburgh, are legendary. The 'Fishwives Causeway' from Portobello remains today as a small remembrance of their once daily journeys. In Peter Anson's (1930s) words, "They did the work of men and had the manners of men in addition to the strength of men"! They played golf and on Shrove Tuesday they held a football match between the married and unmarried women while it was said that in their speech they combined frankness with blunt honesty. The women kept their maiden names long after marrying and controlled the family finances while remaining famously silent, even with husbands, on the subject of their own earnings! Ex-fishwife, Peggy Livingston, remembering back some years ago claimed "When you talk about liberation, here you had a liberated women's society". Appropriately, considering such a proud matriarchal heritage, Scotland's last working fishwife, said to be Betty Millar who retired in 1988, came from Fisherrow.

As the 18th century drew to a close Dunbar could claim, albeit briefly, to be Scotland's second whaling port, with five whalers to Leith's six and Dundee's three. With the first stirrings of the Scottish herring boom beginning, Dunbar seemed perfectly placed. In 1798, 5,000 of the 7,000 barrels of herring exported from Scotland came from here. Yet, as others embraced the industry, Dunbar seemed to decline. Despite this, work on a new harbour basin was begun in 1842 and within two years the Victoria Harbour was completed and declared 'quite magnificent'. It was though, right from the outset, a massive white elephant and nearly bankrupted the town. The entrance was difficult to enter and near impossible in bad weather. As Port Seton and Eyemouth prospered, Dunbar struggled. Herring were landed and cured on broad quaysides but never in the quantities hoped for. By the 1920s, as Mary Johnstone (above with her dog 'Captain') fished from the old pier, Dunbar was in dire straights with just over twenty fishermen left. After the war things improved and, as late as the 1980s, there were still about 30 boats fishing from the town.